THE CHALLENGE OF

Easter

N. T. WRIGHT

IVP Books

An imprint of InterVarsity Press
Downers Grove, Illinois

InterVarsity Press
P.O. Box 1400, Downers Grove, IL 60515-1426
World Wide Web: www.ivpress.com
E-mail: email@ivpress.com

*InterVarsity Press® is the book-publishing division of InterVarsity Christian
Fellowship/USA®, a movement of students and faculty active on campus at
hundreds of universities, colleges and schools of nursing in the United States
of America, and a member movement of the International Fellowship of
Evangelical Students. For information about local and regional activities,
write Public Relations Dept., InterVarsity Christian Fellowship/USA, 6400
Schroeder Rd., P.O. Box 7895, Madison, WI 53707-7895, or visit the IVCF
website at <www.intervarsity.org>.*

*All Scripture quotations, unless otherwise indicated, are the author's
translation.*

Design: Cindy Kiple
Images: iStockphoto

ISBN 978-0-8308-3848-6

Printed in the United States of America ∞

Library of Congress Cataloging-in-Publication Data

Wright, N. T. (Nicholas Thomas)
  The challenge of Easter/N. T. Wright.
    p. cm.
  Adapted from: The challenge of Jesus.
  Includes bibliographical references.
  ISBN 978-0-8308-3848-6 (pbk.: alk. paper)
  1. Jesus Christ—Resurrection. 2. Easter. I. Wright, N. T.
(Nicholas Thomas) Challenge of Jesus. II. Title.
BT482.W74 2009
232.9'7—dc22
                                                              2009034073

P 17 16 15 14 13 12 11 10 9 8 7 6 5 4 3

Y 22 21 20 19 18 17 16 15 14 13 12 11 10

CONTENTS

1

THE QUESTION OF
JESUS' RESURRECTION

At the heart of the Christian faith lies the question of Jesus' resurrection. Why did Christianity arise, and why did it take the shape it did? The early Christians themselves reply: we exist because of Jesus' resurrection.

There is no form of early Christianity known to us—though there are some that have been invented by ingenious scholars—that does not affirm at its heart that after Jesus' shameful death God raised him to life again. Already by the time of Paul, our earliest written witness, the resurrection of Jesus is woven into the very structure of Christian life and thought, informing (among other things) baptism, justification, ethics and the future hope both for humans and for the cosmos.

FALSE TRAILS FROM THE EMPTY TOMB

It has of course been argued, indeed insisted upon, in many circles that whatever we mean by the resurrection of Jesus, it is not accessible to historical investigation. There have been several false trails in the investigation of this question, not least at a popular or semipopular level.

Barbara Thiering proposed that Jesus and the others crucified with him did not die, despite the two others having their legs broken, and that one of them was actually Simon Magus, who was a doctor and had some medicine with him, which he gave to Jesus in the tomb so that he revived and was able to resume his career, traveling around with Paul and the others, not to mention getting married and having children.[1] This is simply a new and highly imaginative twist on an old hypothesis, that Jesus did not really die on the cross. As has been shown often enough, the Romans knew how to kill people, and the reappearance of a battered and exhausted Jesus would hardly be likely to suggest to his followers something for which they were certainly not prepared, namely, that he had gone through death and out the other side.

Equally, there are plenty of people who produce theories to explain that Jesus did not really rise from the dead, leaving an empty tomb behind him. At a popular level, the BBC made a program in the mid-1990s built around the discovery in Jerusalem of an ossuary with the name "Jesus son of Joseph" on it. In the same tomb there were also ossuaries of people named Joseph, Mary, another Mary, a Matthew, and somebody called Judah, described as "son of Jesus." Not surprisingly, among the people who were unimpressed were the Israeli archaeologists, who knew that these names were exceedingly common in the first century. It was rather like finding John and Sally Smith in the London telephone directory.

A book was published in summer 1996 in which two intrepid researchers put together a fast-moving blockbuster of detective research involving the medieval Knights Templar, the Rosicrucians, the Freemasons, the Gnostics, concealed patterns in medieval paintings and so on, all to reach the conclusion that the bones of Jesus are now buried in a hillside in southwestern France, that the real message of the gospel was about living a good life and earning a spiritual, not bodily, resurrection and that the early church made up the doctrine of bodily resurrection as a way to gain political and financial power. The book is called *The Tomb of God*—ironically, because if Jesus' bones are in a tomb in France, there is no reason to suppose that he was or is God. And if they think belief in the resurrection was a way to power or money, they should read the New Testament and think again.

At least these ventures into popular-level pseudo-historiography reveal one thing: the question of Jesus' resurrection remains perennially fascinating, which is good news in an oblique sort of way.

At the more serious scholarly level there has been plenty of continuing discussion of the resurrection. Two writers who do not appear to believe in Jesus' bodily resurrection nevertheless say that something very strange really does seem to have happened. Geza Vermes, in his first book on Jesus, asserts that the tomb really must have been empty, and he does not seem to think that the disciples stole the body.[2] One of the greatest contemporary American writers about Jesus, Ed Sanders, speaks of Jesus' disciples as carrying on the logic of Jesus' own work "in a transformed situation," and says that the result of Jesus' life and work culminated in "the resurrection and the foundation of a movement which endured."[3] Jesus' disciples, he points out, must have been prepared for a dramatic event that would establish the kingdom, but what actually happened—which Sanders describes simply as "the death and resurrection"—"required them to adjust their expectation, but did not create a new one out of nothing."

Both Vermes and Sanders thus bear witness as historians of first-century Judaism to the great difficulty faced by any attempt to say that on the one hand nothing happened to the body of Jesus but that on the other hand Christianity began very soon after his death and began as precisely a resurrection-movement.

Jesus' divinity cannot be the first meaning of his resurrection. The Maccabean martyrs expected to be raised from the dead, but they certainly did not think this would make them divine. Paul argues that all Christians will be raised as Jesus was raised, but he does not suppose that they will thereby share the unique divine sonship that, in the same letter, he attributes to Jesus. Already in Paul, in fact, we see the clear distinction between "resurrection"—a newly embodied life after death—and "exaltation" or "enthronement," a distinction that some scholars have suggested only enters the tradition with Luke.

Let me then treat the resurrection of Jesus as first and foremost a historical problem. There are three stages to this argument, each one of which contains the same four basic steps.[4]

THE KINGDOM OF GOD

The first stage of the argument concerns the rise of Christianity within the Jewish world of its day as a *kingdom-of-God movement*. Already by the time of Paul the phrase "kingdom of God" had become more or less a shorthand for the early Christian movement, its way of life and its raison-d'être. And despite the attempts of some to suggest that this kingdom of God meant for the early Christians a new personal or spiritual experience, rather than a

Jewish-style movement designed to establish the rule of God in the world, all the actual evidence we have—as opposed to the fanciful would-be evidence that some have dreamed up—indicates that if Jesus' movement was a counter-Temple movement, early Christianity was a counter-empire movement. When Paul said "Jesus is Lord," it is clear that he meant that Caesar was not. This is not gnostic escapism but Jewish no-king-but-God theology—with Jesus in the middle of it. And this theology generated and sustained a Jewish new-covenant community. Christianity was indeed, in the Jewish sense, a kingdom-of-God movement.

However, within Judaism the coming kingdom of God was about public events: the end of Israel's exile, the overthrow of the pagan empire and the exaltation of Israel, and the return of YHWH to Zion to judge and save. Looking wider it meant the renewal of the world, the establishment of God's justice for the cosmos. If you had said to some first-century Jews "the kingdom of God is here" and had explained yourself by speaking of a new spiritual experience, a new sense of forgiveness, an exciting reordering of your private religious interiority, they might well have said that they were glad you had had this experience, but why did you refer to it as the *kingdom of God*?

It was abundantly clear that Israel was not liberated, that the Temple was not rebuilt, that evil, injustice, pain and death were still on the rampage. The question presses, then: Why did the early Christians say that the kingdom of God *had* come?

One answer could obviously be: because they changed the meaning of the phrase radically so that it referred not to a political state of affairs but to an internal or spiritual one. But this is simply untrue to early Christianity. In the first written exposition of Christian kingdom-theology, which significantly enough is the same chapter as the first written exposition of the resurrection (1 Cor 15), Paul explained that the kingdom was coming in a two-stage process, so that the Jewish hope—for God to be all in all—would be realized fully in the future, following its decisive inauguration in the events concerning Jesus. The early Christians, in fact, not only used the phrase, but they organized their life as if they really were the returned-from-exile people, the people of the new covenant. They reordered their symbolic world, their story-telling world, their habitual praxis, around it. They acted, in other words, as if the Jewish-style kingdom of God was really present.

Why, in this process, did they *not* continue the sort of kingdom-revolution they had imagined Jesus was going to lead? How do we explain the fact that early Christianity was neither a nationalist Jewish movement nor an existential private experience? The early Christians themselves with one voice say that the reason was the bodily resurrection of Jesus.

THE RESURRECTION

Before exploring this further we must move to the second stage of the argument. Christianity was not just a kingdom-of-God movement; it was, from the first, a *resurrection* movement. There is no evidence for a form of early Christianity in which the resurrection was not a central belief. But what did resurrection mean to a Jew of the first century?

There was a spectrum of views in first-century Judaism concerning what happened to people after their death.

- There are some writings—Philo and the book of Jubilees are examples—that speak of an ultimate nonphysical bliss.

- There are some writings that insist that the physical bodies of at least the righteous dead will be restored so that (for instance) the martyrs will be, as one might say, put back together again to confront their torturers and executioners, and to celebrate their downfall. (The most obvious example of this is 2 Maccabees.)

- There are some writings that speak of a temporary disembodied state, followed by a reembodiment. Wisdom of Solomon 2—3 belongs in this category, despite popular and indeed scholarly assertions that it belongs alongside Philo and Jubilees. This seems to be the position of Josephus, at least when he is taking care to describe what his fellow Jews actually believed as opposed to putting speeches into the mouths of his heroes that he hopes will appeal to his educated Roman audience.

- Finally, there are those who deny that there is any continued existence after death: the Sadducees, notoriously, took this position, though they seem to have left no writings for us to check up on them, so that all we have are reports from people who disagreed with them.

Though there was a range of belief about life after death, the word *resurrection* was only used to describe reembodiment—not the state of disembodied bliss. *Resurrection* was not a general word for "life after death" or for "going to be with God" in some general sense. They could be described as souls, or as angels or some near equivalent, or as spirits, but *not* as resurrected bodies. *Resurrection* was the word for what happened when God created newly embodied human beings after whatever intermediate state there might be.

Resurrection meant reembodiment, but that was not all. From the time of Ezekiel 37 onward "resurrection" was an image used to denote the great return from exile, the renewal of the covenant, and to connote the belief that when this happened it would mean that Israel's sin and death (i.e., exile) had been dealt with, that YHWH had renewed his covenant with his people. Thus the resurrection of the dead became both metaphor and metonymy, both a symbol for the coming of the new age and itself, taken literally, one central element in the package. When YHWH restored the fortunes of his people then of course Abraham, Isaac and Jacob, together with all God's people down to and including the martyrs who had died in the cause of the kingdom, would be reembodied, raised to new life in God's new world.

Thus, if a first-century Jew said that someone had been "raised from the dead," the one thing they did not mean was that such a person had gone to a state of disembodied bliss, there either to rest forever or to wait until the great day of reembodiment. Someone in 150 B.C. who believed passionately that the Maccabean martyrs were true and righteous Israelites, or someone in A.D. 150 who believed that Simeon ben-Kosiba was the true Messiah, might well have said that they were alive in the form of either an angel or a spirit, or that their souls were in the hand of God. But they would not have dreamed of saying that they had been raised from the dead. Resurrection meant embodiment and implied that the new age had dawned.

If, therefore, you had said to a first-century Jew

"the resurrection has occurred," you would have received the puzzled response that it obviously had not, since the patriarchs, prophets and martyrs were not walking around alive again and since the restoration spoken of in Ezekiel 37 had clearly not occurred either. And if by way of explanation you had said that you did not mean that—that you meant, rather, that you had had a wonderful new sense of divine healing and forgiveness or that you believed the former leader of your movement was alive in the presence of God following his shameful torture and death—your interlocutor might have congratulated you on having such an experience but would still have been puzzled as to why you would use the phrase "the resurrection of the dead" to describe either of these things. That simply was not what the words meant.

The very earliest church, however, declared roundly not only that Jesus was raised from the dead but that "the resurrection of the dead" had already occurred (Acts 4:2). What is more, they busily set about redesigning their whole worldview around this new fixed point. That was the inner logic of the Gentile mission, that since God had now done for Israel what he was going to do for Israel, the Gentiles would at last share the blessing. They did not behave as though they had had a new sort of religious experience or as if their former leader was (as the followers of the Maccabean martyrs would no doubt have said of their heroes) alive and well in the presence of God, whether as an angel or a spirit. They behaved, in other words, as though the new age had already arrived—though not in the way that first-century Jews imagined.

Was the early church right? We must postulate something that will account for this group of first-century Jews, including a well-educated Pharisee like Paul, coming so swiftly and so strongly to the conclusion that, against their expectations of *all* the righteous dead being raised to life at the *end* of the present age, *one person* had been raised to life in the *middle* of the present age.

2

PAUL, THE RESURRECTION
AND THE MESSIANIC MOVEMENT

Christianity emerged as a messianic movement with the puzzling difference that, unlike all messianic movements known to us, its Messiah was someone who had already faced the Roman procurator—and had been executed by the Roman troops. We cannot explain the rise of messianic beliefs by the resurrection alone; we must postulate, and the Gospels encourage us to accept, that Jesus acted and spoke messianically during his lifetime and that these actions and words were the proximate cause of his death. But equally we cannot explain why the early church continued to believe that Jesus was the Messiah if he had simply been executed by the Romans in the manner of failed messiahs.

The early church had two normal options open to them. They could have given up messianism, as did the post-A.D. 135 rabbis, and gone in for some form of private religion instead, whether of intensified Torah-observance or something else. They clearly did not do that; anything less like a private religion than going around the pagan world saying that Jesus was the *kyrios kosmou*, the Lord of the world, would be hard to imagine.

Equally and most interestingly the early church could have found themselves a new Messiah from among Jesus' blood-relatives, as with the continuing movement that ran from Judas the Galilean in A.D. 6 through several generations to Eleazar, leader of the ill-fated Sicarii on Masada in 73. We know from various sources that Jesus' relatives continued to be important and well-known within the early church; one of them, James the brother of Jesus, though not having been part of the movement during Jesus' lifetime, became its central figure—the anchorman in Jerusalem while Peter and Paul went off around the world. Yet nobody in early Christianity ever dreamed of saying that James was the Messiah. James was simply known, even to Josephus in *Antiquities* 20, as "the brother of the so-called Messiah."

We are therefore forced once again to postulate something that will explain why this group of first-century Jews, who had cherished messianic hopes and focused them on Jesus of Nazareth, not only continued to believe that he was the Messiah after his death but actively announced him as such in the Jewish as well as the pagan world, cheerfully redrawing the picture of messiahship around him but refusing to abandon it. That is the historical problem of the resurrection of Jesus. And to begin to address the problem, we must turn to our earliest written source: in this case, Paul.

THE RESURRECTED BODY

Paul is the classic example of the early Christian who has woven resurrection so thoroughly into his thinking and practice that if you take it away the whole thing unravels in your hands. We may note further that Paul, as one of the strictest sort of Pharisees, believed passionately in the restoration of Israel and the coming of the new age in which God would judge the world and rescue his people. This is the man we are reading when we turn to 1 Corinthians 15.

We may begin with verse 8. "Last of all, as to one untimely born, he appeared also to me." This is a violent image, invoking the idea of a Caesarian section, in which a baby is ripped from the womb, born before it is ready, blinking in shock at the sudden light, scarcely able to breathe in this new world. We detect here not simply a touch of autobiography as Paul reflects on what it had felt like on the Damascus Road. We trace a clear sense that Paul knew that what had happened to him was precisely *not* like what had happened to the others.

What is more, he only just got in as a witness to the resurrection before the appearances stopped; when he says "last of all," he means that what one might call the ordinary Christian experience of knowing the risen Jesus within the life of the church, of prayer and faith and the sacraments, was not the same sort of thing that had happened to him. He distinguishes his Damascus Road experience, in other words, both from all previous seeings of the risen Jesus and from the subsequent experience of the church, himself included.

Moving back to the start of 1 Corinthians 15, then, we find in verses 1-7 what Paul describes as the very early tradition that was common to all Christians. He received it and handed it on; these are technical terms, and we must assume that this represents what was believed in the very earliest days of the church back in the early 30s. The tradition includes the burial of Jesus (conveniently ignored by Dominic Crossan, who suggests darkly that Jesus' body was eaten by dogs as it hung on the cross so that there was nothing left to bury).[1] In Paul's world, as has been said often enough but still not heard by all scholars, to say that someone had been buried and then raised three days later was to say that the tomb was empty—though the emptiness of the tomb, so important in twentieth-century discussion, was clearly not something that Paul felt the need to stress. For him, saying "resurrection" was quite enough to imply that and much more.

Paul does not, in the list of appearances, mention the appearances to the women. This is not (as is sometimes suggested) because he or the framers of the tradition were chauvinistic, but because this common tradition was designed for use in preaching, where the people listed were clearly regarded as witnesses to the resurrection. In that culture, of course, women were not regarded as reliable witnesses. His mention of the five hundred who saw Jesus at one time cannot be assimilated to the Pentecost-experience mentioned in Acts 2, as some have tried to do, because it precedes the appearance to James, and James was already on board with the early movement by the time of Pentecost.

But perhaps the most important thing about the first paragraph of 1 Corinthians 15 is what Paul understood the resurrection to *mean*. For him it was not a matter of the opening up of a new religious experience. Nor was it a proof of survival, of life after death. It meant that the Scriptures had been fulfilled, that the kingdom of God had arrived, that the new age had broken in to the midst of the present age, had dawned upon a surprised and unready world. It all happened "according to the Scriptures"; the entire biblical narrative had at last reached its climax, had come true in these astonishing events.[2] As a result, Paul can argue that the coming of the new age is a two-stage affair: the Messiah first, then finally the resurrection of all those who belong to the Messiah.

We should note most carefully that the Messiah is not envisaged as being in the present time a soul, a spirit or an angel. He is not in an intermediate state, awaiting a time when he will finally be raised from the dead. He is *already* risen; he is already, as a human being, exalted into the presence of God; he is already ruling the world, not simply in some divine capacity but precisely as a human being, fulfilling the destiny marked out for the human race from the sixth day of creation.[3]

On this basis Paul can move in verses 29-34 to assert most emphatically the future embodiedness both of the Christian dead and of the Christian living, or to put it somewhat more precisely, the future *re*embodiment of the Christian dead and the future *transformed* embodiment of the Christian living. This, he says, is the only explanation within the Jewish worldview, where alone this language makes any sense, for the present practice of the church, both in terms of the strange practice of baptism for the dead and in the more accessible image of his apostolic labors (v. 34, looking on to v. 58). The present life of the church, in other words, is not about "soul-making," the attempt to produce or train disembodied beings for a future disembodied life. It is about working with fully human beings who will be reembodied at the last, after the model of the Messiah.

But what sort of a body will this be? We may jump ahead for a moment to verses 50-57. There Paul states clearly and emphatically his belief in a body that is to be *changed,* not abandoned. The present physicality in all its transience, its decay and its subjection to weakness, sickness and death, is not to go on and on forever; that is what he means by saying "flesh and blood cannot inherit the kingdom of God." For Paul "flesh and blood" does not mean "physicality" per se but the corruptible and decaying present state of our physicality. What is required is what we might call a "noncorruptible physicality": the dead will be raised "incorruptible" (v. 52), and we—that is, those who are left alive until the great day—will be changed.

This is not mere resuscitation, but equally it is emphatically not disembodiment. And if this is what Paul believes about the resurrection body of Christians, we may assume (since his argument works from the one to the other) that this was his view of the resurrection of Jesus as well.

In verses 35-49 Paul speaks of the future resurrection body as a "spiritual body." He does *not* mean, as has often been suggested, a "nonphysical" body. To say that is to allow into the argument a Hellenistic worldview that is quite out of place in this most Jewish of chapters. He is contrasting the present body, which is a *soma psychikon,* with the future body, which is a *soma pneumatikon.*

Soma means "body," but what do the two adjectives mean? Here the translations are often quite unhelpful, particularly RSV and NRSV with their misleading rendering of "physical body" and "spiritual body." Since *psyche,* from which *psychikon* is derived, is regularly translated "soul," we might as well have assumed that Paul thought that the present body too was nonphysical! Since that is clearly out of the question, we are right to take both phrases to refer to an actual physical body, animated by "soul" on the one hand and "spirit"—clearly God's spirit—on the other. The present body, Paul is saying, is "a [physical] body animated by 'soul'"; the future body is "a [transformed physical] body animated by God's Spirit."

Paul, then, writing in the early 50s and claiming to represent what the whole main stream of the church believed, insisted on certain things about the resurrection of Jesus.

1. It was the moment when the creator God fulfilled his ancient promises to Israel, saving them from "their sins," their exile. It thus initiated the "last days," at the end of which the victory over death begun at Easter would at last be complete.

2. It involved the transformation of Jesus' body: it was, that is to say, neither a resuscitation of Jesus' dead body to the same sort of life nor an

abandonment of that body to decomposition. Paul's account presupposes the empty tomb.

3. It involved Jesus' being seen alive in a very limited early period, after which he was known as present to the church in a different way. These early sightings constituted those who witnessed them as apostles.[4]

4. It was the prototype for the resurrection of all God's people at the end of the last days.

5. It was thus the ground not only for the future hope of Christians but for their present work.

3

THE GOSPEL ACCOUNTS

As we turn our gaze wider toward the rest of the New Testament and early Christianity we find Paul's perspective reaffirmed at every turn. The resurrection narratives of the Gospels, for all their puzzling nature and apparent conflicts, are quite clear on three points.

First, the sightings of and meetings with Jesus are quite unlike the sort of heavenly visions or visions of a figure in blinding light or dazzling glory or wreathed in clouds that one might expect in the Jewish apocalyptic or mystical traditions. The portrait of Jesus himself in these stories does not appear to have been modeled on existing stories of "supernatural appearances." It was not created out of expectation alone.

Second, the body of Jesus seems to be both physical, in the sense that it was not a nonmaterial angel or spirit, and transphysical, in the sense that it could come and go through locked doors. As I read the Gospel accounts, I have a sense that they are saying, in effect, "I know this is extraordinary, but this is just how it was." They are, in effect, describing more or less exactly that for which Paul provides the underlying theoretical framework: an event for which there was no precedent and of which there remains as yet no subsequent example, an event involving neither the resuscitation nor the abandonment of a physical body, but its transformation into a new mode of physicality.

Third, the accounts are quite clear that the appearances of Jesus were not the sort of thing that went on happening during the continuing existence of the early church. Luke did not suppose that his readers might meet Jesus on the road to Emmaus. Matthew did not expect his audience to meet him on a mountain. John did not suppose that people were still liable to come upon Jesus cooking breakfast by the shore. Mark certainly did not expect his readers to "say nothing to anyone, for they were afraid."

All attempts to show that the resurrection narratives in the Gospels are derived from other literature have conspicuously failed. Meanwhile, it is often noted that the tomb of Jesus was not venerated in the manner of the tombs of the martyrs, that we have to explain the emphasis in very early Christianity on the first day of the week as the Lord's Day.

It is not so often pointed out that the burial of Jesus was intended as the first part of a two-stage burial; had his body been still in a tomb somewhere, someone would sooner or later have had to collect the bones and put them in an ossuary, and the game would have been up. These and similar considerations force the eye back to the first Easter day and to the question we have asked all along: what precisely happened?

ALTERNATIVE THEORIES

Among those who deny the bodily resurrection of Jesus, one theory is particularly common—that Peter and Paul experienced some sort of visionary hallucination. Peter, they say, was overcome with grief and perhaps guilt, and experienced what people in that state often do: a sense of the presence of the lost person with him, talking to him, reassuring him. Paul, they say, was in a state of fanatical guilt, and this induced a similar fantasy in him. The two of them then communicated their experience enthusiastically to the other disciples, who underwent a kind of corporate version of the same fantasy.

This theory is not new, though it has been revived in new ways. But I have to say that as a historian I find such theories far harder to accept than the stories told by the evangelists themselves, for all their problems. For a start, if Peter or Paul had had such experiences, the category that would have suggested itself would not be "resurrection"; it would be that of the appearance of Jesus' "angel" or his "spirit."[1] We had better learn to take seriously the witness of the entire early church, that Jesus of Nazareth was raised bodily to a new sort of life, three days after his execution.

It is this, of course, that offers far and away the best explanation of the rise of that same early church. All other explanations leave far more questions unsolved than solved. In particular, it explains why the church came so very early to believe that the new age had dawned; why, in consequence, they came to believe that Jesus' death had not been a messy accident, the end of a beautiful dream, but rather the climactic saving act of the God of Israel, the one God of all the earth; and why, in consequence, they—to their own astonishment—arrived at the conclusion that Jesus of Nazareth had done what, according to the Scriptures, only Israel's God could do.

In that sense the resurrection pointed them toward that full christology that they came to hold within twenty or so years. But the critical thing right from the beginning was that the resurrection of Jesus demonstrated that he was indeed the Messiah, that Jesus had indeed borne the destiny of Israel on his shoulders in carrying the Roman cross outside the city walls, that he had gone through the climax of Israel's exile and had returned from that

exile three days later according to and in fulfill-
ment of the entire biblical narrative, and that his
followers in being the witnesses to these things
were thereby and thereupon commissioned to take
the news of his victory to the ends of the earth.

THE FIRST DAY

When we put Jesus firmly and clearly into his own
first-century Jewish context, and see how his message related uniquely and specifically to that situation, it seems much harder to get any sense of his
relevance for today. If we believe in any sense that
Jesus is the light of the world, how do we move
from looking at Jesus and seeing the challenge he
posed to his contemporaries, to shedding the light
of this same Jesus on our own world? How do we
come to terms with the challenge that faces us, that
of relating the true Jesus to our own tasks and
equally that of facing today's world with the challenge of Jesus?

The first thing to do is to grasp the full significance of the bodily resurrection. We have far too
often flattened out the resurrection into meaning
simply that there is life after death. Or we have seen
its significance simply in the fact that Jesus is alive
today, and we can get to know him. That is glori-
ously true, but it is not the specific truth of Easter
itself. The many-sided truth of Easter is set out in
many passages in the New Testament but emerges

particularly in John's Gospel. And in John 20:1, 19, John tells us quite plainly: Easter day is the first day of the week.

John doesn't waste words. When he tells us something like this twice, he knows what he's doing. It isn't just that Easter day happened to be on a Sunday. John wants his readers to figure out that Easter day is the first day of God's new creation. Easter morning was the birthday of God's new world.

On the sixth day of the week, the Friday, God finished all his work. The great shout of *tetelestai*, "It is finished!" in John 19:30 looks all the way back to the sixth day in Genesis 1 when, with the creation of human beings in his own image, God finished the initial work of creation. John then invites us to see the Saturday, the sabbath between Good Friday and Easter day, in terms of the sabbath rest of God after creation was done:

> On the seventh day God rested
> in the darkness of the tomb;
> Having finished on the sixth day
> all his work of joy and doom.
> Now the word had fallen silent,
> and the water had run dry,
> The bread had all been scattered,
> and the light had left the sky.
> The flock had lost its shepherd,

and the seed was sadly sown,
The courtiers had betrayed their king,
and nailed him to his throne.
O Sabbath rest by Calvary,
O calm of tomb below,
Where the grave-clothes and the spices
cradle him we did not know!
Rest you well, beloved Jesus,
Caesar's Lord and Israel's King,
In the brooding of the Spirit,
in the darkness of the spring.

The Spirit who brooded over the waters of creation at the beginning broods now over God's world, ready to bring it bursting to springtime life. Mary goes to the tomb while it's still dark and in the morning light meets Jesus in the garden. She thinks he is the gardener, as in one important sense he indeed is. This is the new creation. This is the new Genesis.

On the first day of the week, then, in the evening when the doors were shut for fear, Jesus came and stood in the midst and said, "Peace be with you." With the new creation, a new order of being has burst upon the startled old world, opening up new possibilities. And the message that accompanies this is the age-old Jewish message of *shalom,* "peace"—not just a standard greeting but deeply indicative again of the achievement of the cross, as

John at once indicates: "Saying this, Jesus showed them his hands and his side."

With this comes (Jn 20:19-23) the commission, the word that stands at the head of all Christian witness, mission, all discipleship, all reshaping of our world. "Peace be with you," he said again; "as the Father sent me, so I send you." And he breathed on them as once, long ago, God had breathed into the nostrils of Adam and Eve his own breath, his breath of life. Receive the Holy Spirit. Forgive sins and they are forgiven; retain them and they are retained.

It is this three-sided commissioning that I want to explore now as we look at Jesus as the light of the world, the challenge that faces every generation. The three sides are these:

1. as the Father sent me, so I send you;
2. receive the Holy Spirit;
3. forgive sins and they are forgiven, retain them and they are retained.

4

THE LIGHT OF THE WORLD

The whole New Testament assumes that Israel was chosen to be the people through whom the creator God would address and solve the problems of the whole world. Salvation is of the Jews. The early Christians believed that the one true God had been faithful to that promise and had brought salvation through the king of the Jews, Jesus himself. Israel was called to be the light of the world; Israel's history and vocation had devolved on to Jesus, solo. He was the true Israel, the true light of the whole world.

AS THE FATHER SENT ME
But what did it mean to be the light of the world? It meant, according to John, that Jesus would be lifted up to draw all people to himself. On the cross Jesus would reveal the true God in action as the lover and savior of the world. It was because Israel's history

with God and God's history with Israel came to its climax in Jesus, and because Jesus' story reached its climax on Calvary and with the empty tomb, that we can say: here is the light of the world. The Creator has done what he promised. From now on we are living in the new age, the already-begun new world. The light is now shining in the darkness, and the darkness has not overcome it.

This means that the church, the followers of Jesus Christ, live in the bright interval between Easter and the final great consummation. Let's make no mistake either way. The reason the early Christians were so joyful was because they knew themselves to be living not so much in the *last* days (though that was true too) as in the *first* days—the opening days of God's new creation. What Jesus did was not a mere example of something else, not a mere manifestation of some larger truth; it was itself the climactic event and fact of cosmic history. From then on everything is different.

But it would be equally mistaken to forget that after Easter, after Pentecost, after the fall of Jerusalem, the final great consummation is still to come. Paul speaks of this in Romans 8 and 1 Corinthians 15: the creation itself will receive its exodus, will be set free from its slavery to corruption, death itself will be defeated, and God will be all in all. Revelation 21 speaks of it in terms of new heavens and new earth.[1]

In all of these scenarios the most glorious thing is of course the personal, royal, loving presence of Jesus himself. I still find that among the most moving words I ever sing in church are those in the old Christmas carol "Once in Royal David's City":

And our eyes at last shall see him,
Through his own redeeming love.

Blessed, says Jesus, are those who have not seen yet believe; yes, indeed, but one day we shall see him as he is and share the completed new creation that he is even now in the process of planning and making. We live, therefore, between Easter and the consummation, following Jesus Christ in the power of the Spirit and commissioned to be for the world what he was for Israel, bringing God's redemptive reshaping to our world.

Christians have always found it difficult to understand and articulate this, and have regularly distorted the picture in one direction or the other. Some suppose God will simply throw the present world in the trash can and leave us in a totally different sphere altogether. There is then really no point in attempting to reshape the present world by the light of Jesus Christ. Armageddon is coming, so who cares about acid rain or third-world debt?

That is the way of dualism; it is a radically anti-creation viewpoint and hence is challenged head on by (among many other things) John's emphasis on Easter as the first day of the new week, the start of God's new creation.

On the other hand, some have imagined we can actually build the kingdom of God by our own hard work. This is sorely mistaken. When God does what God intends to do, this will be an act of fresh grace, of radical newness. At one level it will be quite unexpected, like a surprise party with guests we never thought we would meet and delicious food we never thought we would taste. But at the same time there will be a rightness about it, a rich continuity with what has gone before so that in the midst of our surprise and delight we will say, "Of course! This is how it had to be, even though we'd never imagined it."

SO I SEND YOU

Right at the end of 1 Corinthians 15, in verse 58, Paul says something that could seem like an anticlimax. Rather than a shout of praise at the glorious future that awaits us, which would be appropriate, Paul writes: "Therefore, my beloved family, be steadfast, immovable, always abounding in the work of the Lord, inasmuch as you know that in the Lord your labor is not in vain."

What is he saying? Just this: that part of the point of bodily resurrection is that there is vital and important *continuity* as well as discontinuity between this world and that which is to be, precisely because the new world has already begun with Easter and Pentecost, and because everything done on the basis of Jesus' resurrection and in the power of the Spirit already belongs to that new world. It is already part of the kingdom-building that God is now setting forward in this new week of new creation.

That is why Paul speaks in 1 Corinthians 3:10-15 of Jesus as the foundation and of people building on that foundation with gold, silver or precious stones, or as it may be, with wood, hay and stubble. If you build on the foundation in the present time with gold, silver and precious stones, *your work will last*. In the Lord your labor is not in vain. You are not oiling the wheels of a machine that is soon going over a cliff.

Nor, however, are you constructing the kingdom of God by your own efforts. You are following Jesus and shaping our world in the power of the Spirit. And when the final consummation comes, the work that you have done—whether in Bible study or biochemistry, whether in preaching or in pure mathematics, whether in digging ditches or in composing symphonies—will stand, will last.

The fact that we live between, so to speak, the beginning of the End and the end of the End, should enable us to come to terms with our vocation to be for the world what Jesus was for Israel, and in the power of the Spirit to forgive and retain sins. The foundation Paul writes of in 1 Corinthians 3 is unique and unrepeatable. If you try to lay a foundation again you are committing apostasy.

The church has so often read the Gospels as the teaching of timeless truths that it has supposed that Jesus did something for his own day, and that we simply have to do the same—to teach the same truths or to live the same way for our own day. Jesus, on this model, gave a great example; our task is simply to imitate him. By itself that is a radical denial of the Israel-centered plan of God and of the fact that what God did in Jesus the Messiah was unique, climactic and decisive. People who think like that sometimes end up making the cross simply the great example of self-sacrificial love instead of the moment within history when the loving God defeated the powers of evil and dealt with the sin of the world, with our sin, once and for all. That is, once more, to make the gospel good advice rather than good news.

Before you can say "as Jesus to Israel, so the church to the world," you have to say *"because* Jesus to Israel, *therefore* the church to the world." What Jesus did was unique, climactic, decisive.

RECEIVE THE SPIRIT
But once the foundation is laid, it does indeed provide the pattern, the shape, the basis for a building to be constructed. Our task is to *implement* Jesus'

unique *achievement*. We are like the musicians called to play and sing the unique and once-only-written musical score. We don't have to write it again, but we have to play it. Or, in the image Paul uses in 1 Corinthians 3, we are now in the position of young architects discovering a wonderful foundation already laid by a master architect and having to work out what sort of a building was intended. Clearly he intended the main entrance to be here; the main rooms to be on this side, with this view; a tower at this end; and so on. When you study the Gospels, looking at the unique and unrepeatable message, challenge, warning and summons of Jesus to Israel, you are looking at the unique foundation upon which Jesus' followers must now construct the kingdom-building, the house of God, the dwelling place for God's Spirit.

In case anyone should think this is all too arbitrary, too chancy, we are promised at every turn that the Spirit of the master architect will dwell in us, nudging and guiding us, correcting mistakes, warning of danger ahead, enabling us to build—if only we will obey—with what will turn out to have been gold, silver and precious stones. "As the Father sent me, so I send you; . . . receive the Holy Spirit." These two go together. Just as in Genesis, so now in the new Genesis, the new creation, God breathes into human nostrils his own breath, and we become living stewards, looking after the garden, shaping God's world as his obedient im-age-bearers. Paul, indeed, uses the image of the gar-dener alongside that of the builder in 1 Corinthians 3. We are to implement Jesus' unique achievement.

This perspective should open the Gospels for us in a whole new way. Everything that we read there tells us something about the foundation upon which we are called to build. Everything, therefore, gives us hints about what sort of a building it is to be. As Jesus was to Israel, so the church is to be for the world.

But, you say, the people we minister to, the peo-ple we work with in the laboratory or the fine arts department, the people who serve us in the grocery store or who work in the power station, are not first-century Jews. How can we summon them as Jesus summoned his contemporaries? How can we challenge them in the same way? What is the equiv-alent? What is the key to help us to translate Jesus' message into our own?

The key is that humans are made in the image of God. That is the equivalent, on the wider canvas, of Israel's unique position and vocation. And bearing God's image is not just a fact, it is a vocation. It means being called to reflect into the world the cre-ative and redemptive love of God. It means being made for relationship, for stewardship, for wor-ship—or, to put it more vividly, for sex, gardening and God.

Human beings know in their bones that they are made for each other, made to look after and shape this world, made to worship the one in whose image they are made. But like Israel with her vocation, we get it wrong. We worship other gods and start to reflect their likeness instead. We distort our vocation to stewardship into the will to power, treating God's world as either a gold mine or an ashtray. And we distort our calling to beautiful, healing, creative many-sided human relationships into exploitation and abuse.

Marx, Nietzsche and Freud described a fallen world in which money, power and sex have become the norm, displacing relationship, stewardship and worship. Part of the point of postmodernity under the strange providence of God is to preach the Fall to arrogant modernity. What we are faced with in our culture is the post-Christian version of the doctrine of original sin: all human endeavor is radically flawed, and the journalists who take delight in pointing this out are simply telling over and over again the story of Genesis 3 as applied to today's leaders, politicians, royalty and rock stars.

Our task, as image-bearing, God-loving, Christ-shaped, Spirit-filled Christians, following Christ and shaping our world, is to announce redemption to the world that has discovered its fallenness, to announce healing to the world that has discovered its brokenness, to proclaim love and trust to the world that knows only exploitation, fear and suspicion.

Humans were made to reflect God's creative stewardship into the world. Israel was made to bring God's rescuing love to bear upon the world. Jesus came as the true Israel, the world's true light, and as the true image of the invisible God. He was the true Jew, the true human. He has laid the foundation, and we must build upon it. We are to be the bearers both of his redeeming love and of his creative stewardship: to celebrate it, to model it, to proclaim it, to dance to it.

5

RETAINING
AND FORGIVING SINS

God intends to do through us for the wider world that for which the foundation was laid in Jesus. We are to live and tell the story of the prodigal and the older brother; to announce God's glad, exuberant, richly healing welcome for sinners, and at the same time God's sorrowful but implacable opposition to those who persist in arrogance, oppression and greed. Following Christ in the power of the Spirit means bringing to our world the shape of the gospel: forgiveness, the best news that anyone can ever hear, for all who yearn for it; and judgment for all who insist on dehumanizing themselves and others by their continuing pride, injustice and greed.

The human race has been in exile; exiled from the garden, shut out of the house, bombarded with noise instead of music. Our task is to announce in deed and word that the exile is over, to enact the symbols that speak of healing and forgiveness, to act boldly in God's world in the power of the Spirit. Luther's definition of sin was *homo incurvatus in se*, "humans turned in on themselves." Does the industry in which you find yourself foster or challenge that? You may not be able to change the way your discipline currently works, but that isn't necessarily your vocation. Your task is to find the symbolic ways of doing things differently, planting flags in hostile soil, setting up signposts that say there is a different way to be human. And when people are puzzled at what you are doing, find ways—fresh ways—of telling the story of the return of the human race from its exile, and use those stories as your explanation.

At the risk of trespassing in areas I know little or nothing about, let me simply hint at some ways in which this might work out. If you work in information technology, is your discipline slanted toward the will to power or the will to love? Does it exhibit the signs of technology for technology's sake, of information as a means for the oppression of those who do not have access to it by those who do? Is it developing in the service of true relationships, true stewardship and even true worship, or is it feeding and encouraging a society in which everybody creates their own private, narcissistic, enclosed world?

Or suppose you work in fine art or music or architecture. Is your discipline still stuck in the arrogance of modernity? Or more likely, is it showing all the signs of the postmodern fragmentation, the world that declares that all great stories, all overarching systems, are power plays? Is your discipline run by people with a strong political agenda so that (say) unless you are a committed Marxist they don't think you can be a serious artist? Your calling may be to find new ways to tell the story of redemption, to create fresh symbols that will speak of a home for the homeless, the end of exile, the replanting of the garden, the rebuilding of the house.

I knew a young artist who became a Christian at Oxford and struggled with tutors who despised him for it. His answer, to his own surprise, was to start painting abstract icons. They were spectacular and deeply beautiful. He didn't tell his tutors what they were until they had expressed their surprise and delight at this new turn in his work, drawing forth from him quite fresh creativity which they could not help but admire. Then when they asked what was going on, he told them the story.

So we could go on. If you are to shape your world in following Christ, you are called, prayerfully, to discern where in your discipline the human project is showing signs of exile and humbly and boldly to act symbolically in ways that declare that the powers have been defeated, that the kingdom has come in Jesus the Jewish Messiah, that the new way of being human has been unveiled, and to be prepared to tell the story that explains what these symbols are all about. And in all this you are to declare, in symbol and practice, in story and articulate answers to questions, that Jesus is Lord and Caesar is not; that Jesus is Lord and Marx, Freud and Nietzsche are not; that Jesus is Lord and neither modernity nor postmodernity is. When Paul spoke of the gospel, he was not talking primarily about a system of salvation but about the announcement, in symbol and word, that Jesus is the true Lord of the world, the true light of the world.

I am well aware that all this may seem like a counsel of perfection. People in every walk of life have legitimate and appropriate goals, and they need to pay their dues, to live humbly within their chosen sphere in order to attain those goals. There is a danger in Christians supposing that they simply have to be flaky, awkward, against the government all the time, continually doing things upside down and inside out. Some people of course seem to be born that way, and use the gospel imperative as an excuse for foisting their own cussedness or arrogance on everyone else. There is a need for wisdom. There is a time to speak and a time to remain silent. If it is worth working within a discipline in the first place, that is probably because there is a good deal of it that is healthy, important and to be supported.

But as you pray about your work, and as in your church you and your fellow Christians are regularly planting the main symbols of the kingdom—by which I mean of course the sacraments and the inclusive family life of the people of God—you may gradually discern a sense of new things that can be done, new ways of going about your tasks. Do not despise the small but significant symbolic act. God probably does not want you to reorganize the entire discipline or the entire world of your vocation overnight. Learn to be symbol-makers and story-tellers for the kingdom of God. Learn to model true humanness in your worship, your stewardship, your relationships. The church's task in the world is to model genuine humanness as a sign and an invitation to those around.

CROSS-BEARING

As with Jesus' kingdom-announcement, this task will involve retaining sins as well as forgiving them. It will involve declaring that those who persist in dehumanizing and destructive ways of going about their human tasks and goals are calling down destruction on themselves and their world. If only you had known, said Jesus, the things that make for peace! If only you had known, we must sometimes say in symbol and word, the things that make for peace, for stewardship, for justice, for love, for trust. But if you don't, your project is heading for disaster.

Now, I don't recommend that a graduate student should say this to their advisory panel or tenure committee. I don't recommend it as a line to use in a job interview. There is a real danger here that Christians who have not actually done the hard work or thought through the issues will hide their incompetence behind a cheap dismissal of their academic or professional superiors as dehumanizing non-Christians. That might of course be a true assessment, but it might also be the mere sour grapes of disappointed ambition. If you have ears, then hear.

But if we are to be kingdom-announcers, modeling the new way of being human, we are also to be crossbearers. This is a strange and dark theme that is also our birthright as followers of Jesus. Shaping our world is never for a Christian a matter of going out arrogantly thinking we can just get on with the job, reorganizing the world according to some model that we have in mind. It is a matter of sharing and bearing the pain and puzzlement of the world so that the crucified love of God in Christ may be brought to bear healingly upon the world at exactly that point. Because Jesus bore the cross uniquely for us, we do not have to purchase forgiveness again; it's been done. But because, as he himself said, following him involves taking up the cross, we should expect, as the New Testament tells us repeatedly, that to build on his foundation will be to find the cross etched into the pattern of our life and work over and over again.

We would rather this were not so, and we twist and turn to avoid it. We find ourselves in Gethsemane, saying, "Lord, can this really be the way? If I have been obedient so far, why is all this happening to me? Surely you don't want me to be feeling like this?"

Sometimes, indeed, the answer may be "No." It is possible that we have indeed taken a wrong road and must now turn and go by a different way. But often the answer is simply that we must stay in Gethsemane. The way of Christian witness is being in Christ, in the Spirit, at the place where the world is in pain, so that the healing love of God may be brought to bear at that point.

This perspective is deeply rooted in New Testament theology, not least in Romans 8. There Paul speaks of the whole creation groaning together in travail. Where should the church be at such a time? Sitting smugly on the sidelines, knowing it's got the answers? No, says Paul: we ourselves groan too, because we too long for renewal, for final liberation. And where is God in all this? Sitting up in heaven wishing we could get our act together? No, says Paul (Rom 8:26-27): God is groaning too, present within the church at the place where the world is in pain. God the Spirit groans within us, calling in prayer to God the Father.

The Christian vocation is to be in prayer, in the Spirit, at the place where the world is in pain, and as we embrace that vocation, we discover it to be the way of following Christ, shaped according to his messianic vocation to the cross, with arms outstretched, holding on simultaneously to the pain of the world and to the love of God.

Paul, we should note carefully, is quite clear about one thing: as we embrace this vocation, the prayer is likely to be inarticulate. It does not have to be a thought-out analysis of the problem and the solution. It is likely to be simply a groan, a groan in which the Spirit of God, the Spirit of the crucified and risen Christ, groans within us, so that the achievement of the cross might be implemented afresh at that place of pain, so that the music of the cross might be softly sung at that place of pain, so that the foundation of the cross might support a new home at that place of exile.

So if you are a Christian who works in government or foreign policy or finance or economics or business, you will be wrestling with the issues, often in a Gethsemane-like anguish in which the pain of the world and the healing love of God are brought together in inarticulate prayer. How much easier to say you're just a private Christian and hope things will work out somehow, or to embrace a shrill and shallow agenda that has not taken seriously the depth of the problem. Some readers of this book will be called to live in that Gethsemane so that the healing love of God may reshape our world at a crucial and critical time.

I have known faculties where half the professors are Marxists and half are not, or where half are committed postmodernists and half are not. Where should the Christian be in such a case? You may well believe that the gospel commits you to one side in the debate, though these things are rarely that easy. But my suggestion is that you see it as a call to be in prayer where your discipline is in pain. Read the Scriptures on your knees with your discipline and its problems on your heart. Come to the Eucharist and see in the breaking of the bread the broken body of Christ given for the healing of the world. Learn new ways of praying with and from the pain, the brokenness, of that crucial part of the world where God has placed you. And out of that prayer discover the ways of being peacemakers, of taking the risk of hearing both sides, of running the risk of being shot at from both sides. Are you or are you not a follower of the crucified Messiah?

Of course this applies in many other areas as well: in families and marriages, in public policy and private dilemmas. I have had a very clear vocation that has resulted in some very unclear choices. I live in a world that has done its best, since the Enlightenment, to separate the church from the academy. I believe passionately that this is deeply dehumanizing in both directions, and I have lived my adult life with a foot on both sides of the divide, often misunderstood by both. I live in a world where Christian devotion and evangelical piety have been highly suspicious of and sometimes implacably opposed to serious historical work on the New Testament, and vice versa. I believe passionately that this is deeply destructive of the gospel, and I have done my best to preach and to pray as a serious historian and to do my historical work as a serious preacher and pray-er. This has resulted in some fellow-historians calling me a fundamentalist and some fellow-believers calling me a compromised pseudo-liberal. The irony does not make it any less painful.

I am not looking for sympathy in saying all this. In my experience it has been precisely when I have found myself in prayer on one of those fault-lines in another private Gethsemane (and sometimes they have been moments of real agony) that I have known the presence and comfort of the living Messiah, that I have discovered that the one with whom I was wrestling and who has left me limping was none other than the angel of the Lord, and I have been reassured again and again that my calling is not necessarily to solve the great dualities of our post-Enlightenment and now postmodern world, but to live in prayer at the places where the world is in pain, in the assurance that through this means—

at a level far deeper than the articulate solving of
the problem—my discipline may find new fruitful-
ness and my church, perhaps, new directions. And
out of that may perhaps grow, I pray, work that is
peacemaking and fruitful.

I hesitate to hold myself up as a model, but it
may be that my experience will resonate with
some others who read these words and perhaps
bring encouragement to some for whom Gethsemane has been hitherto an unnamed and hence
misunderstood reality. "As the Father sent me,"
said Jesus, "so I send you; receive the Holy Spirit;
forgive and retain sins." We need to reflect long
upon, and to be prepared to live with, the meaning of that "as . . . so."

TRULY HUMAN

And of course, if we are faithful and loyal to this
calling, the most frightening and unexpected thing
of all, at least within many Protestant and evangelical traditions, is that we will in turn be for the world
not only what Jesus was for Israel but what YHWH
was and is for Israel and the world. If you believe in
the presence and power of the Holy Spirit in your
life, this is what it means. You are called to be truly
human, but it is nothing short of the life of God
within you that enables you to be so, to be remade
in God's image. As C. S. Lewis said in a famous lec-
ture, next to the sacrament itself your Christian

neighbor is the holiest object ever presented to your sight, because in him or her the living Christ is truly present.[1]

We do not normally think of it like this, and we impoverish ourselves hugely as a result. We are so concerned to say at once, if anyone even suggests such an idea, that we are imperfect, weak and frail, that we fail and sin and fear and fall. And of course all that is true. But read Paul again, read John again, and discover that we are cracked vessels full of glory, wounded healers. God forgive us that we have imagined true humanness, after the Enlightenment model, to mean being successful, having it all together, knowing all the answers, never making mistakes, striding through the world as though we owned it. The living God revealed his glory in Jesus and never more clearly than when he died on the cross, crying out that he had been forsaken. When we stand in pain and prayer, following Christ and reshaping our world, we are not only discovering what it means to be truly human, we are discovering the true meaning of what the Eastern Orthodox Church refers to as "divinization."

Ultimately, if you don't believe that, you don't believe in the Holy Spirit. And if you think that sounds arrogant, imagine how arrogant it would be even to think of trying to reshape our world *without* being indwelt, energized, guided and directed by God's own Spirit. Once you realize that true divinity is revealed not in self-aggrandizement, as the Enlightenment supposed, but in self-giving love, you realize that when you worship the God revealed in Jesus and so come to reflect that God more and more, the humility of God and the nobility of true humanness belong together.

TRUE KNOWING

In and through all of this, we are called to true *knowing*. All Christians, whatever their vocation, are called to knowledge of God, of themselves, of one another, of the world. It is true that the much-vaunted objectivism of the Enlightenment ("we're just looking at things straight; we're just telling it like it is") was often a camouflage for political and social power and control. But when all is said and done, it is part of the essential human task given in Genesis and reaffirmed in Christ that we should *know* God, that we should know one another, that we should know God's world. Paul speaks of being "renewed in *knowledge* after the image of the creator" (Col 3:10). And this knowledge is far more than mere guesswork that is always in danger of being deconstructed.

Current accounts of knowing have placed the would-be objective scientific knowing (test-tube epistemology, if you like) in a position of privilege. Every step away from this is seen as a step into obscurity, fuzziness and subjectivism, reaching its peaks in aesthetics and metaphysics. That is why, for instance, people have often asked me when I have spoken about Jesus whether I am really saying that Jesus did not "know" he was God. My answer to that is that if by "know" you mean what the Enlightenment meant, no, he did not. He had something much richer and deeper instead.

We dare not, as Christians, remain content with an epistemology wished upon us from one philosophical and cultural movement, part of which was conceived in explicit opposition to Christianity. One aspect of following Jesus the Messiah is that we should allow our knowledge of him, and still more his knowledge of us, to inform us about what true knowing really is. I believe that a biblical account of "knowing" should follow the great philosopher Bernard Lonergan and take *love* as the basic mode of knowing, with the love of God as the highest and fullest sort of knowing that there is, and should work, so to speak, down from there.[2]

I believe we can and must, as Christians within a postmodern world, give an account of human knowing that will apply to music and mathematics, to biology and history, to theology and to chemistry. We need to articulate, for the post-postmodern world, what we might call an epistemology of love. This is at the heart of our great opportunity, here and now, for serious and joyful Christian mission to the postpostmodern world.

We live at a time of cultural crisis. At the moment I don't hear anyone out there pointing a way forward out of the postmodern morass; some people are still trying to put up the shutters and live in a premodern world, many are clinging to modernism for all they're worth, and many are deciding that living off the pickings of the garbage heap of postmodernity is the best option on offer. But we can do better than that. It isn't simply that the gospel of Jesus offers us a religious option that can outdo other religious options, that can fill more effectively the slot labeled "religion" on the cultural and social smorgasbord. The gospel of Jesus points us and indeed urges us to be at the leading edge of the whole culture, articulating in story and music and art and philosophy and education and poetry and politics and theology and even, heaven help us, biblical studies, a worldview that will mount the historically rooted Christian challenge to both modernity and postmodernity, leading the way into the postpostmodern world with joy and humor and gentleness and good judgment and true wisdom.

I believe we face the question: If not now, then when? And if we are grasped by this vision, we may also hear the question: If not us, then who? And if the gospel of Jesus is not the key to this task, then what is? "As the Father sent me, so I send you; receive the Holy Spirit; forgive and retain sins."

In October 1998 my wife and I went to Paris for a

conference, and in a spare moment we visited the Louvre. It was the first time either of us had been there. A disappointment awaited us: the Mona Lisa, which every good tourist goes to goggle at, is not only as enigmatic as she has always been but following a violent attack is now behind thick glass. All attempts to look into those famous eyes, to face the famous questions as to what they are meaning and whether this meaning is really there or is being imposed by the viewers, are befogged by glimpses of other eyes—one's own, and dozens more besides—reflected back from the protective casing. Ah, says postmodernity, that's what all of life is like. What seems like knowledge is really the reflection of your own ideas, your own predispositions or inner world. You can't trust anything; you have to be suspicious of everything.

But is that true? I believe, and I challenge my readers to work this out in their own worlds, that there is such a thing as a love, a knowing, a hermeneutic of trust rather than suspicion, which is what we most surely need for the twenty-first century:

A Paris newcomer, I'd never been
Followed by those dark eyes, bewitched by
    that
Half-smile. Meaning, like beauty, teases,
    dancing
In the soft spaces between portrait, artist,

And the beholder's eye. But now, twice shy,
She hides behind a veil of wood and glass;
And we who peer and pry into her world
See cameras, schoolchildren, other eyes,
Other disturbing smiles. So, now, we view
The world, each other, God, through prison
　　glass:
Suspicion, fear, mistrust—projections of
Our own anxieties. Is all our knowing
Only reflection? Let me trust, and see,
And let love's eyes pursue, and set me free.

Notes

Chapter 1: The Question of Jesus' Resurrection

[1]Barbara Thiering, *Jesus the Man* (New York: Bantam, 1994). Her more recent venture in the same genre, *The Book That Jesus Wrote* (New York: Bantam, 1998), proposes that Jesus himself was the author of John's Gospel.

[2]Geza Vermes, *Jesus the Jew: A Historian's Reading of the Gospels* (London: Collins, 1973), pp. 37-41.

[3]E. P. Sanders, *Jesus and Judaism* (Philadelphia: Fortress; London: SCM Press, 1985), pp. 320, 340.

[4]I have spelled this argument out more fully in two articles in the *Sewanee Theological Review* 41, no. 2 (1998): 107-40.

Chapter 2: Paul, the Resurrection and the Messianic Movement

[1]John Dominic Crossan, *Jesus: A Revolutionary Biography* (San Francisco: HarperSanFrancisco, 1994), chap. 6.

[2]See N. T. Wright, *The New Testament and the People of God* (Minneapolis: Augsburg Fortress, 1992), pp. 241-43.

[3]This is the significance of Paul's quotation, in 15:27, of Psalm 8:6 ("God has put all things in subjection under his feet").

[4]Cf. 1 Cor 9:1.

Chapter 3: The Gospel Accounts

[1]Cf. Acts 12:15; 23:8-10.

Chapter 4: The Light of the World

[1]See N. T. Wright, *New Heavens, New Earth: The Biblical Picture of Christian Hope,* Grove Biblical Series 11 (Cambridge: Grove, 1999).

Chapter 5: Retaining and Forgiving Sins

[1]C. S. Lewis, "The Weight of Glory," in *Screwtape Proposes a Toast and Other Pieces.*

[2]On Bernard Lonergan see the writings of Ben F. Meyer, particularly *The Aims of Jesus* (Philadelphia: Fortress, 1978); and *Critical Realism and the New Testament* (Allison Park, Penn.: Pickwick, 1989).

The Challenge of Easter is excerpted and adapted from *The Challenge of Jesus: Rediscovering Who Jesus Was and Is* (Downers Grove, Ill.: InterVarsity Press, 1999). The implications of the resurrection of Jesus, described and discussed here, are further explored in that book, as well as in other books by Bishop Wright, including *The Resurrection of the Son of God* (volume 3 of Christian Origins and the Question of God [Minneapolis: Augsburg Fortress, 2003]) and *Surprised by Hope: Rethinking Heaven, the Resurrection, and the Mission of the Church* (San Francisco: HarperOne, 2008).